Fern Green
photographs by Deirdre Rooney

hachette
AUSTRALIA

CONTENTS

INTRODUCTION

We all know protein is essential for our body, as are carbohydrates and fats, and we are aware that you can get a lot of protein from eating meat. But what you may not know is that you can also get proteins from plants, which have great health benefits.

Whether you are a vegetarian or vegan and want to find out more about getting protein in your diet, or perhaps you feel you want to eat less meat, this book aims to give you confidence in eating green proteins.

What is protein?

Proteins are made up of 22 amino acids. These help form enzymes, hormones, antibodies and new tissues in our body, and are important for our skin, muscles, tendons, cartilage, hair and nails.

There are two groups of amino acids, 'essential' which are derived from what we eat, and 'non-essential' which can be made by our bodies. Nearly all foods that are not processed or refined contain protein. This essential protein contains all protein-forming amino acids in some quantity, and it is these that you need a variety of in your diet.

Types of protein

Animal
Animal proteins contain all the essential amino acids that we need. These are found in meat, poultry, fish, eggs and dairy products.

Plant (green)
Plant proteins contain many amino acids but not one contains all of them. These are found in legumes, cereals, beans, grains, nuts, seeds and soy products. You need to combine different green proteins to make up the complete range of amino acids needed by your body.

Green versus animal

To maintain a healthy diet, there are many reasons why we should aim to have more green protein than animal protein. Animal products are good sources of protein but unfortunately they can also be high in saturated fat and cholesterol. We tend to use fatty products like butter to enhance flavour in animal products, which leads to an increase in fat and cholesterol.

Plant proteins are low in fat and high in fibre. They also contain lots of vitamins and minerals, thus improving immune function and helping to protect against cancer. They help reduce cholesterol and blood sugar levels, which lowers the risk of heart disease and they also contain phytochemicals that contribute towards disease prevention and overall health. For example, edamame beans have antioxidant properties, which are important in reducing menopausal symptoms.

The delicious recipes in this book aim to show you that by eating a variety of plant foods you can easily get enough protein to have a healthy, balanced diet.

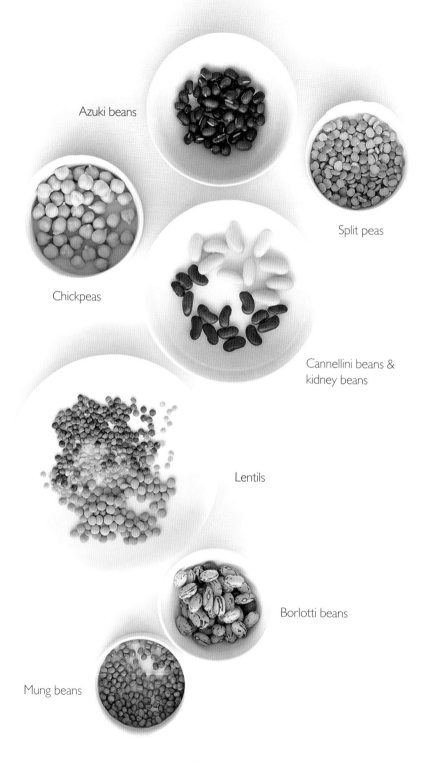

Azuki beans

Split peas

Chickpeas

Cannellini beans &
kidney beans

Lentils

Borlotti beans

Mung beans

THE BEST GREEN PROTEINS

- Chickpeas
- Split peas
- Lentils
- Cannellini and kidney beans
- Borlotti beans
- Azuki beans
- Mung beans
- Broad beans

- Quinoa
- Edamame
- Tempeh
- Soy milk
- Tofu
- Nuts and seeds
- Germinating seeds – sprouts

Chickpeas – 8.86g protein per 100g

Buy them dried, already cooked or as a flour. If dried soak overnight, drain and boil for 30–40 minutes.
Health benefits: High in fibre, reduces cholesterol and risk of heart disease.

Split peas – 25g protein per 100g

Boil split peas for 20 minutes–1 hour.
Health benefits: Helps stabilise blood sugar level and very high in fibre.

Lentils – 26g protein per 100g

Lentils take 10–40 minutes to cook.
Health benefits: High in magnesium, high in fibre and aids digestion.

Cannellini beans and kidney beans – 22.3g and 24g protein per 100g

These common beans are high in starch, protein and fibre. They are often sold dried as well as cooked.
Health benefits: Helps stabilise blood sugar level, full of antioxidants which protect your skin.

Borlotti beans – 23g protein per 100g

Soak borlotti beans for 12 hours, then drain and boil for 1 hour.
Health benefits: Helps stabilise blood sugar level, provides a wide range of B vitamins, iron, potassium and zinc.

Azuki beans – 17.3g protein per 100g

Soak dried beans for 2 hours, or overnight; drain and boil for 1 hour.
Health benefits: Helps improve digestion and stabilise cholesterol, also said to lower the risk of getting breast cancer among women.

Mung beans – 23.86g protein per 100g

This Indian native bean is often soaked before boiling for 45 minutes.
Health benefits: Helps with weight loss as it is rich in fibre and reduces cholesterol level.

Edamame

Tempeh

Tofu

Soy milk

Nuts & seeds

Quinoa

Broad beans – 7.9g protein per 100g

Sometimes called fava beans, buy fresh or dried; the dried beans are best bought split without the hard skins. Soak for 12 hours, then drain and cook for 40–60 minutes.

Health benefits: A very good source of iron and folate, they are also low in fat, high in protein and rich in dietary fibre.

Quinoa – 8g protein per 100g

Most grains contain a small amount of protein but this South American grain, which is technically a seed, has all nine of the essential amino acids needed for growth and repair. Toast it for a few minutes in a dry pan, then add 675ml liquid for every 300g quinoa and cook for 15 minutes for plump, dry grains.

Health benefits: High in fibre and iron; contains lysine which is essential for tissue growth and repair.

Edamame – 10.88g protein per 100g

Like any other bean, soybeans contain rich amounts of fibre, carbohydrate, magnesium and folates. Sprinkle with salt or add to salads and rice dishes.

Health benefits: High in fibre, a great immune booster and high in manganese, which is a good for building strong bones.

Tempeh – 18g protein per 100g

Tempeh is often soaked, marinated and fried then served in salads, sandwiches and stews. It is commonly used as a meat replacement.

Health benefits: Reduces cholesterol.

Soy milk – 2.86g protein per 100g

Produced by soaking dry soybeans and grinding them with water, it is very popular in Asia instead of cow's milk. It contains the same proportion of protein and has little saturated fat and no cholesterol.

Health benefits: Reduces cholesterol.

Tofu – 8g protein per 100g

Also called bean curd, tofu is sold in different textures, depending on what has been added to it: soft silken tofu, firm tofu and extra firm tofu. It is often highly flavoured with spices and salt products and braised or fried to give it a crispy texture.

Health benefits: Reduces cholesterol.

Nuts and seeds – 20–30g protein per 100g

As well as being high in protein, they are rich in folate, fibre and minerals such as magnesium and selenium.

Health benefits: Full of healthy heart fat, energy providing and it contains powerful minerals.

Here is how:

Put 2 handfuls of seeds, grains or beans in a bowl. Cover with water and let them soak overnight.

The next day, rinse thoroughly and place them into a clean bowl. Cover loosely with damp kitchen paper and rinse each morning until you see the sprouts. This should take between 2–4 days.

They are ready when the sprout is about 2.5cm in length. Keep in the fridge ready to consume and sprinkle over salads when needed.

SPROUTING SEEDS, GRAINS & BEANS

Seeds, grains and beans can take on a different nutritional value when they have been sprouted. They can have up to 100 times more enzymes than raw vegetables, which add more vitamins and minerals into our diet. You can sprout quinoa to mung beans, alfalfa to sunflower seeds, azuki beans to lentils . . . the list goes on. Please note that nuts and flaxseeds don't sprout.

This chart is a rough guide to how long different varieties of seeds, grains and beans need to soak, and how long their sprouting time is.

FOOD	SOAKING TIME (HOURS)	SPROUTING TIME (DAYS)
Azuki beans	10	4
Barley	6	2
Black beans	10	3
Buckwheat	6	2–3
Chickpeas	8	2–3
Kamut	7	2–3
Lentils	7	2–3
Millet	5	12 hours
Mung beans	8–12	4
Pumpkin seeds	8	3
Radish seeds	8–12	3–4
Sesame seeds	8	2–3
Sunflower seeds	8	12–24 hours
Quinoa	4	2–3
Wheat berries	7	3–4
Wild rice	9	3–5

HOW TO MAKE A GREEN PROTEIN RECIPE

This is not a definitive guide but a way to give you confidence to create flavours and textures in your very own green protein recipe. First, choose your green protein, then decide what type of dish you want. Next, start thinking of flavours, whether you would like to go Mediterranean or spicy. Choose your vegetables to complement each other and think about adding a dressing or sauce. Add a chopped herb or two, then finally, add texture, such as something crunchy.

1. CHOOSE A GREEN PROTEIN			2. CHOOSE A DISH	3. CHOOSE A FEW VEGETABLES
Grain	**Legumes**	**Soy product**		
Quinoa	Chickpeas	Edamame	Starter	Artichoke
Bulgur wheat	Split peas	Tempeh	Sandwiches/	Asparagus
Farro/Spelt	Broad beans	Soy milk	Snacks	Avocado
Brown rice	Lentils	Tofu	Soup	Beetroot
Barley	Cannellini		Salad	Broccoli
Couscous	beans		Small hot dish	Cabbage
(wholewheat)	Kidney beans		Casseroles	Capsicum
	Borlotti beans			Carrot
	Azuki beans			Cauliflower
	Mung beans			Celeriac
				Celery
				Chard
				Cucumber
				Eggplant
				Fennel
				Green peas
				Kale
				Lettuce
				Mushrooms
				Parsnip
				Potato & sweet potato
				Pumpkin
				Spinach
				Sugar snap peas
				Sweetcorn
				Tomato

4. ADD A DRESSING, SAUCE OR OTHER INGREDIENTS FOR FLAVOUR		5. ADD FRESH HERBS	6. ADD TEXTURE
Salty / spicy	**Sweet / tangy**	**Herbs**	**Nuts, seeds & sprouts**

Mediterranean
Capers
Feta
Garlic
Anchovies
Olives
Parmesan
 	
Asian
Miso
Soy
Seaweed
Red or green chilli
Kimchi
Black/Pink
  peppercorns
 	
Middle Eastern
Preserved lemons
Olives
Harissa
Tahini
	Mediterranean
	Lemons
	Raisins
	Balsamic vinegar
	Honey/Maple
	  syrup
	
	Asian
	Mirin
	Rice vinegar
	
	Middle Eastern
	Dates
	Plain yoghurt
	Pomegranate
	  molasses
	Lemons
	Honey/Maple
	  syrup
		Mediterranean
		Thyme
		Oregano
		Marjoram
		Basil
		Mint
		Rosemary
		Chives
		Parsley
		Dill
		
		Asian
		Coriander
		Parsley
		Asian basil
		Mint
		
		Middle Eastern
		Parsley
		Mint
		Dill
			Mediterranean
			Almond
			Pine nut
			Walnut
			Hazelnut
			Pistachio
			Flaxseeds
			Hemp
			Pumpkin
			
			Asian
			Peanut
			Brazil nut
			Cashew
			Coconut
			Pecan
			Sesame
			Sunflower
			Chia seed
			
			Middle Eastern
			Almond
			Hazelnut
			Walnut
			Sesame
			
			Sprouts
			From lentils/beans
			  and quinoa

SNACKS, SANDWICHES & STARTERS

Colourful small bites of food that you can have on the go, as well as sharing with your friends at home. From falafels and bruschetta ideas, to pizzas, wraps and pancakes.

Coriander hummus • Quinoa cakes with lemon yoghurt • Warm broad bean dip • Lentil & basil bruschetta • Azuki bean & seaweed croquettes Dry-roasted edamame • Orange & ginger tempeh Sweet potato falafels • Chickpea pancakes Borlotti beans on toast • Vegetable spiced tempeh wrap • Tempeh rice paper rolls • Curried tofu scramble tortilla • Chickpea flatbread pizza

CORIANDER HUMMUS

Serves: 4 - Time: 25 minutes–1 hour 25 minutes, plus soaking overnight (optional)

YOU NEED

250g dried chickpeas or 2 x 400g cans chickpeas

1 teaspoon bicarbonate of soda • 1 small potato, peeled and quartered

5 handfuls of spinach • 1 small red onion • 1 teaspoon coriander seeds,
toasted then ground • grated zest and juice of 1 lemon • 1 teaspoon salt, plus extra
salt and pepper to taste • 180ml extra virgin olive oil

60ml rapeseed or groundnut oil • 1 spring onion, finely sliced

If using dried chickpeas, soak them overnight with the bicarbonate of soda. Drain, bring to the boil then simmer for 1 hour. Add the potato and cook for 10 minutes, then drain. Whizz the chickpeas, potato, spinach, onion, coriander seeds, lemon zest and half the lemon juice in a food processor. Add 1 teaspoon salt and both oils, then whizz and season with salt and pepper to taste. Add lemon juice to loosen. Sprinkle with spring onion.

QUINOA CAKES WITH LEMON YOGHURT

Serves: 4 - Time: 40 minutes, plus 1 hour chilling

YOU NEED
2 handfuls of spinach leaves • 1 garlic clove, grated
200g quinoa, cooked • 1 large egg • 60g parmesan cheese, grated
1 teaspoon paprika • ½ teaspoon ground cumin • ½ teaspoon cumin seeds
2 tablespoons olive oil • juice of 1 lemon • salt and pepper to taste

---

LEMON HERB YOGHURT SAUCE
100ml plain yoghurt • 1 tablespoon lemon juice
1 teaspoon chopped chives • 2 teaspoons chopped parsley

Cook the spinach with the garlic until it wilts. Cool. Combine the remaining cake ingredients with the spinach. Season with salt and pepper to taste, mix and chill for 1 hour. Make 6 patties from the mixture and fry for 4 minutes on each side. Combine the sauce ingredients, season and serve with the cakes.

WARM BROAD BEAN DIP

Serves: 4 - Time: 1 hour 20 minutes, plus soaking overnight

YOU NEED

300g dried broad beans • 130ml extra virgin olive oil
40ml groundnut oil • 1 red onion, finely chopped • 2 garlic cloves, chopped
½ teaspoon ground cumin • ½ teaspoon ground coriander
¼ teaspoon cayenne pepper • 120ml lemon juice • 2 medium tomatoes, seeded
and roughly chopped • 3 spring onions, finely sliced • salt and pepper to taste
1 tablespoon chopped mint • 1 tablespoon chopped coriander

CRISPY ONIONS

1 red onion, finely sliced • 1 teaspoon yellow mustard seeds

26g
protein /
per serving
5.3g

Soak the beans overnight then drain and rinse. Skin, bring to the boil then
simmer for 30 minutes. Drain and set aside. Fry the red onion, garlic and spices
in 2 tablespoons of olive oil for 2 minutes. Add the beans and mash. Add the
lemon juice, 40ml olive oil, the groundnut oil, the tomatoes and spring onions
and cook for 2 minutes. Season with salt and pepper and add the herbs. Fry the
onion and mustard seeds in the remaining olive oil in 4 batches for 5 minutes
each. Drain on kitchen paper, then serve the dip with the onions on top.

LENTIL & BASIL BRUSCHETTA

Serves: 2 - Time: 25 minutes

YOU NEED

100g cooked green lentils • a handful of baby spinach or rocket, torn
a handful of basil leaves, torn • 1 tablespoon chopped flat-leaf parsley
1 garlic clove, grated • ½ lemon, plus ½ lemon, to finish • 100ml Greek yoghurt
salt and pepper to taste • 30g pine nuts, toasted and roughly chopped
30ml extra virgin olive oil • 2 slices sourdough bread, toasted
10g parmesan cheese, grated (optional)

46g
protein /
per serving
23g

Combine the lentils, spinach, basil, parsley and garlic. Squeeze the lemon and fold in the yoghurt. Add salt and a lot of pepper. Fold in the chopped nuts and put on top of the toasted bread. Drizzle with the oil, sprinkle over the grated parmesan, if using, and squeeze over the remaining lemon juice.

AZUKI BEAN & SEAWEED CROQUETTES

Serves: 4 - Time: 2 hours 5 minutes, plus overnight soaking

YOU NEED

185g dried azuki beans • 2 tablespoons dry white wine
1 tablespoon sesame oil, plus extra for brushing • 5cm piece dried wakame
seaweed • 1 medium onion, stuck with 2 cloves • 4 garlic cloves
5cm piece ginger, grated • 2 dried whole red chillies • 2 bay leaves
1 teaspoon soy sauce • 4 spring onions, roughly chopped • a pinch of sea salt
1 teaspoon ground black pepper • 90g breadcrumbs • 120g sesame seeds, toasted

---

SAUCE

90ml tamari • 2 tablespoons rice vinegar • 1 tablespoon sesame oil
1 tablespoon toasted sesame oil • 1 tablespoon maple syrup • ½ teaspoon cayenne
pepper • 1 garlic clove, grated • 2.5cm piece ginger, peeled and grated

46g
protein /
per serving
11.5g

Soak the beans overnight, then drain and rinse. Put the beans in a pan with
1 litre water, wine, oil, seaweed, onion, garlic, ginger, chillies and bay leaves.
Bring to the boil then simmer for 1 hour. Drain, remove the vegetables and add
the soy sauce. Preheat the oven to 200°C/400°F. Whizz the beans with the
spring onions, salt, pepper and breadcrumbs. Roll into sausages then lightly
oil with sesame oil and roll in the sesame seeds. Bake for 20 minutes. Mix all
the sauce ingredients together, including 90ml warm water, then heat
and serve.

DRY-ROASTED EDAMAME

Serves: 4 - Time: 30 minutes

YOU NEED

300g frozen edamame beans, defrosted • 2 teaspoons olive oil

1 teaspoon soy sauce • 1 teaspoon black sesame seeds

1 teaspoon white sesame seeds

36g
protein /
per serving
8g

Preheat the oven to 230°C/450°F and line a baking tray with baking paper.
Combine the beans with the oil and soy sauce. Spread onto the baking tray
and bake for 12–15 minutes. Sprinkle the sesame seeds over and bake for a
further 5 minutes. Keep an eye on them to make sure the seeds do not burn.
Remove from the oven and leave until they are cool enough to handle.

ORANGE & GINGER TEMPEH

Serves: 4 - Time: 35 minutes

YOU NEED

120ml fresh orange juice • 1 thumb-sized piece ginger, peeled and grated

1 teaspoon soy sauce • 1 tablespoon mirin • 1 teaspoon maple syrup

a pinch of ground coriander • 1 garlic clove, grated

140g tempeh, sliced into matchsticks • 1 tablespoon olive oil

1 carrot, cut into julienne • 8 baby gem lettuce leaves

a handful of coriander, chopped • ½ lime

25g
protein /
per serving
6.25g

Combine the orange juice, ginger, soy, mirin, maple syrup, coriander and garlic. Mix together and set aside. Fry the tempeh in the oil for 5 minutes, add the carrot and fry for 4 minutes. Pour the orange mixture into the pan and simmer for 10 minutes. Trim the lettuces and pull off the leaves. Spoon a little tempeh mixture on top, sprinkle with coriander, squeeze the lime over and serve.

SWEET POTATO FALAFELS

Makes: 12–15 - Time: 40 minutes

YOU NEED

4 sweet potatoes, pricked • 400g can chickpeas, drained and rinsed
2 tablespoons chickpea (besan) flour • 1 teaspoon ground cumin
1 teaspoon ground coriander • 2 teaspoons smoked paprika
grated zest and juice of 1 lemon • salt and pepper to taste • 40g parmesan, grated
2 tablespoons olive oil • a handful of mint, chopped • 100ml plain yoghurt

52.2g
protein /
per serving
13g

Microwave the sweet potatoes for 10 minutes in a 850W oven. If your microwave
has a higher wattage, cook them for less time. Cool then scoop out the flesh
and put in a food processor with the chickpeas, flour, spices and lemon zest.
Season with salt and pepper and whizz, then form into small quenelles.
Grind pepper into the parmesan then roll the quenelles in the mix. Fry the
quenelles in oil for 4–6 minutes until brown. Drain on kitchen paper. Combine
the lemon juice, mint and yoghurt and serve with the falafels.

CHICKPEA PANCAKES

Makes about 15–20 tiny pancakes - Time: 35 minutes

YOU NEED
90g chickpea (besan) flour • ¾ teaspoon salt • 1 large egg
120ml buttermilk • 30ml extra virgin olive oil • 1 tablespoon black sesame seeds
½ teaspoon yellow mustard seeds • ½ tablespoon olive oil, for frying

---

RAITA
2 mint sprigs, roughly chopped • 100ml plain yoghurt • 1 green chilli, sliced
1 red onion, finely diced

Whisk the flour, salt, eggs, 120ml water, buttermilk, 30ml extra virgin olive oil,
sesame seeds and mustard seeds together until smooth. Leave for 15 minutes,
then stir. Combine the raita ingredients and reserve. Heat the remaining oil,
add a tablespoon of batter to the frying pan and fry for 1–2 minutes each side,
or until lightly golden, then transfer to kitchen paper. Repeat 3–4 times to
make the other pancakes. Serve with the raita.

BORLOTTI BEANS ON TOAST

Serves: 2 - Time: 1 hour 15 minutes, plus overnight soaking

YOU NEED

90g dried borlotti beans • 3 garlic cloves • 1 celery stick
½ red onion, halved • 1 ripe tomato • 40ml extra virgin olive oil
salt and pepper to taste • 4 large sage leaves • 2 slices sourdough bread

Soak the beans overnight, then drain and rinse. Put the beans in a pan with
1 garlic clove, the celery, onion and tomato. Cover with water and add 2
tablespoons of the oil, then cover with a lid. Bring to the boil then simmer for
30 minutes. Uncover and simmer for another 30 minutes, adding 125–225ml
more water if necessary to stop them drying out. Remove the celery, onion and
tomato and season with salt and pepper. Fry the sage in 1 tablespoon of oil
until crispy; set aside. Chargrill the sourdough. Rub with the remaining garlic,
then add the cooked beans, drizzle the rest of the oil over the top and add the
crispy sage leaves.

VEGETABLE SPICED TEMPEH WRAP

Serves: 2 - Time: 30 minutes, plus 20 minutes marinating

YOU NEED

125g tempeh, sliced and cubed • 1 carrot, cut into julienne
½ celery stick, cut into julienne • ½ red capsicum, seeded and sliced lengthways
½ small orange, peeled and sliced • salt and pepper to taste
2 wholemeal tortilla wraps • a handful of baby spinach

MARINADE

1 teaspoon chilli powder • 2 tablespoons lemon juice • 1 teaspoon smoked paprika
1 teaspoon honey • 2 tablespoons olive oil

DRESSING

2 tablespoons tahini • 2 tablespoons cider vinegar • 1 teaspoon honey

27g
protein /
per serving
13.5g

Combine the marinade ingredients, add the tempeh and marinate for 20 minutes. Mix together the dressing ingredients, stir in the carrot, celery and capsicum, mash in the orange, mix and season with salt and pepper. Fry the tempeh with the marinade for 2 minutes. In the wraps, add a layer of spinach then the vegetables, then the tempeh. Fold the wrap, slice and serve.

39

TEMPEH RICE PAPER ROLLS

Makes 8 rolls - Time: 45 minutes

YOU NEED

115g tempeh, cut into 5mm slices, then cut into 5mm matchsticks
8 rice paper wrappers • ½ large carrot, grated • 25g iceberg lettuce, shredded
¼ cucumber, cut into julienne • 25g frozen edamame beans, defrosted
20g beansprouts • a few mint, basil and coriander leaves

MARINADE

1 tablespoon soy sauce • ½ tablespoon sesame oil
½ teaspoon Sriracha chilli sauce • ½ tablespoon vegetable oil

---

DIPPING SAUCE

2 garlic cloves, grated • ½ red chilli, seeded and chopped
2 teaspoons honey • juice of 1 lime • 3 tablespoons fish sauce

Combine the marinade ingredients, add the tempeh and leave for 5 minutes. Sear the tempeh with the marinade in a frying pan. Put the rice paper wrappers, 2 or 3 at a time, into a bowl of slightly warm water until soft. Lift them out and let them dry a little. Put the tempeh, carrot, lettuce, cucumber, beans, beansprouts and a few herb leaves in the centre of the wrappers. Roll up tightly around the filling, tucking in the sides as you go. Combine the dipping sauce ingredients and serve.

CURRIED TOFU SCRAMBLE TORTILLA

Serves: 4 - Time: 15 minutes

YOU NEED
240g extra firm tofu • 1 red onion, finely chopped
½ teaspoon chilli powder • 1 tablespoon vegetable oil
1 green chilli, finely chopped • 1 tomato, seeded and finely chopped
a handful of baby spinach leaves • 4 small corn tortillas
a handful of coriander, roughly chopped

25g
protein /
per serving
6.3g

Mash the tofu. Fry the onion with the chilli powder in the oil for 2 minutes.
Add the green chilli and tomato and fry for 1 minute. Add the tofu and fry for
2 minutes then add the spinach and cook until wilted. Warm the tortillas in
the microwave for 10 seconds and serve the scramble on top of each tortilla,
sprinkled with coriander.

CHICKPEA FLATBREAD PIZZA

Serves: 4 - Time: 30 minutes

YOU NEED
120g chickpea (besan) flour

1½ tablespoons extra virgin olive oil, plus extra for drizzling

40g parmesan, grated • 1 tablespoon thyme leaves • 1 tablespoon basil, torn

salt and pepper to taste • 1 buffalo mozzarella, sliced • rocket, to garnish

---

CASHEW PESTO
150g cashew nuts • a handful of fresh basil leaves

a large handful of baby spinach leaves • juice of ½ lemon

4 tablespoons extra virgin olive oil • 4 tablespoons rapeseed or groundnut oil

82.5g protein / per serving 20.7g

Preheat the oven to 240°C/450°F and oil a 22 or 24cm cake tin. Whizz all the pesto ingredients together in a food processor. Season with salt and pepper. Sift the flour, whisk in 1 cup water and the oil. Add the parmesan, herbs, seasoning and whisk to combine. Pour the batter into the cake tin and bake for 15 minutes. Spread with the pesto, add the mozzarella, top with rocket and a drizzle of olive oil.

SOUPS
& SALADS

Vibrant vegetables and grains that make warm delicious soups, along with crunchy salads packed full of goodness and punchy flavours that will keep your hunger at bay as well as give you the energy you need.

Pasta & chickpea soup • Broccoli & split pea soup
Coconut red lentil soup • Azuki bean & Swiss chard
soup • Pea & edamame soup • Salmon, tofu & chive
soup • Tofu, seaweed & lemongrass broth • Spring
green chickpea salad • Zucchini quinoa salad
Hazelnut, lentil & avocado salad • Asian azuki &
mung bean salad • Azuki bean & quinoa tabbouleh
Edamame & barley salad • Pistachio-crusted tofu
Tofu, eggplant & chilli salad • Japanese tuna rice
salad • Avocado & almond farro salad

PASTA & CHICKPEA SOUP

Serves: 4 - Time: 2 hours 45 minutes, plus soaking overnight (optional)

YOU NEED

110g dried chickpeas or 400g canned • 1 medium carrot, finely diced
1 celery stick, finely diced • 1 onion, finely diced • 1 tablespoon olive oil
2 tablespoons tomato purée • 1 rosemary sprig • 500ml vegetable or chicken stock
1 parmesan rind, plus extra grated cheese for sprinkling • salt and pepper to taste
225g small dried tubular pasta, cooked to al dente • a small handful of parsely,
chopped, to serve

If using dried chickpeas, soak overnight, then drain and rinse. Put in a pan,
cover with water and bring to the boil, then simmer for 2 hours until tender.
Drain. Fry the carrot, celery and onion in the oil until soft. Add the tomato purée
and rosemary, stir, then add two-thirds of the chickpeas. Stir then cover with
stock and add the parmesan rind. Boil then simmer for 20 minutes. Remove
the rind and rosemary, and blend until smooth. Add the remaining chickpeas
and season with salt and pepper. Add the pasta and sprinkle with grated
parmesan and chopped parsley.

BROCCOLI & SPLIT PEA SOUP

Serves: 4 - Time: 2 hours

YOU NEED

2 onions, roughly chopped • 1 tablespoon olive oil, plus extra for drizzling

360g dried split green peas • 1.2 litres vegetable stock

½ broccoli head, florets halved, plus 1 extra floret, chopped into tiny pieces

juice of ½ lemon • salt and pepper to taste

28g
protein /
per serving
7g

Fry the onions in the oil until soft. Add the split peas and stock, boil then simmer for 1½ hours. Preheat the oven to 200°C/400°F. Add the broccoli to the soup and simmer for 5–6 minutes. Drizzle the extra chopped broccoli with oil, sprinkle with salt and roast for 6 minutes. Purée the soup and add lemon juice to taste. Season with salt and pepper and sprinkle the roasted broccoli on top to serve.

COCONUT RED LENTIL SOUP

Serves: 4 - Time: 45 minutes

YOU NEED

150g yellow split peas • 150g red split lentils

1 medium carrot, cut into small chunks • 2 tablespoons grated ginger

2 tablespoons garam masala • 1 teaspoon ground cumin

1 tablespoon olive oil • 5 spring onions, thinly sliced • 3 tablespoons tomato purée

400ml can coconut milk • 50g golden raisins • salt and pepper to taste

---

TO GARNISH

a handful of coriander, roughly chopped

desiccated coconut, toasted • 1 red chilli, sliced

27.8g
protein /
per serving
7g

Put the peas, lentils and 1.2 litres water in a large pan. Bring to the boil, then simmer and add the carrot and half the ginger. Cover and cook for 30 minutes. Fry the garam masala and cumin in the oil for 1 minute. Add the spring onions, remaining ginger and tomato purée and cook for 2 minutes. Add this mixture to the peas. Add the coconut milk and raisins and simmer for 20 minutes. Season with salt and pepper, garnish and serve.

AZUKI BEAN & SWISS CHARD SOUP

Serves: 4 - Time: 1 hour 30 minutes, plus soaking overnight

YOU NEED

250g dried azuki beans • 1 onion, roughly chopped • 2 carrots, roughly chopped
1 celery stick, sliced • 1 tablespoon olive oil • 2 garlic cloves, sliced • 1 bay leaf
1 tablespoon ground cumin • 1 tablespoon smoked paprika
2 tablespoons tomato purée • 400g can chopped tomatoes • 1 teaspoon honey
90g quinoa • 180g Swiss chard, roughly chopped • salt and pepper to taste
1 tablespoon oregano, roughly chopped

24.5g
protein /
per serving
6.1g

Soak the beans overnight, then drain and rinse. Fry the onion, carrots and celery in the oil over a low heat for 10 minutes. Add the garlic, bay leaf and spices and cook for 3 minutes. Stir in the tomato purée, then add the tomatoes and cook for 5 minutes. Pour in 1.8 litres water, then add the soaked beans. Bring to the boil then simmer for 1 hour. In the last 15 minutes of cooking, add the honey, quinoa and Swiss chard. Season with salt and pepper to taste, stir in the oregano and serve.

PEA & EDAMAME SOUP

Serves: 4 - Time: 40 minutes

YOU NEED

1 onion, finely chopped • 1 green chilli, seeded and finely chopped

1 medium potato, peeled and cubed • 1 tablespoon olive oil

500g frozen edamame beans, defrosted • 100g frozen peas, defrosted

200g baby spinach leaves • 1.2 litres vegetable stock • salt and pepper to taste

black sesame seeds and sesame oil, to garnish

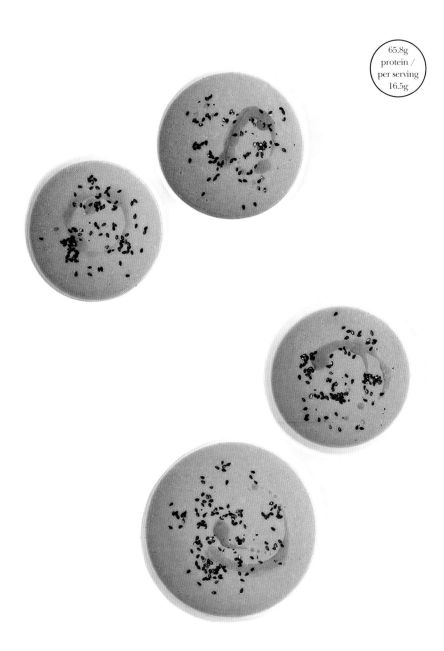

65.8g
protein /
per serving
16.5g

Fry the onion, chilli and potato in the oil for 4 minutes until soft. Add the beans, peas, spinach and stock. Cover and simmer for 20 minutes. Season with salt and pepper then blend the soup. Garnish with sesame seeds and sesame oil.

SALMON, TOFU & CHIVE SOUP

Serves: 4 - Time: 45 minutes

YOU NEED

1.2 litres chicken stock • 1 thumb-sized piece of ginger, peeled and sliced
2 garlic cloves, chopped • a handful of coriander, chopped, stalks kept
300g raw salmon, cubed • 200g tofu, cubed • 5 spring onions, finely sliced
1 teaspoon soy sauce • juice of 1 lime • a handful of chives, chopped

Boil the stock with the ginger, garlic and coriander stalks, then simmer for
30 minutes. Strain. Return the stock to the boil, add the salmon, tofu, spring
onions, soy and lime juice and simmer for 1 minute. Top with chives and
coriander leaves.

TOFU, SEAWEED & LEMONGRASS BROTH

Serves: 4 - Time: 30 minutes

YOU NEED

1 lemongrass stalk, finely sliced • 1 tablespoon grated ginger
1 teaspoon grated garlic • 1 red chilli, chopped • 1 tablespoon olive oil
400–500ml vegetable stock • 400g can coconut milk
20g seaweed, cut into squares • 5 button mushrooms, sliced
115g firm tofu, cubed • 1 teaspoon soy sauce • juice of 1 lime
½ teaspoon brown sugar • salt and pepper to taste
a handful of coriander leaves, roughly chopped

Stir-fry the lemongrass, ginger, garlic and chilli in the oil for a minute. Add
the stock and coconut milk and simmer for 15 minutes. Add the seaweed,
mushrooms, tofu and soy sauce. Stir in the lime juice and sugar and season with
salt and pepper to taste. Sprinkle with coriander.

SPRING GREEN CHICKPEA SALAD

Serves: 4 - Time: 1 hour, plus soaking overnight

YOU NEED

185g dried chickpeas • 1 teaspoon bicarbonate of soda

150g garden peas • a handful of mint • a handful of dill

a handful of parsley • 2 preserved lemons, flesh removed • 50g plain yoghurt

1 tablespoon extra virgin olive oil • 1 teaspoon lemon juice

1 teaspoon maple syrup • a pinch of salt

2 teaspoons chopped mint, dill and parsley

18.5g
protein /
per serving
4.6g

Soak the dried chickpeas overnight, then drain and rinse. Put the chickpeas and bicarbonate of soda in a pan, bring to the boil then simmer for 40 minutes. Cook the peas, then refresh under cold water. Whizz the herbs, preserved lemon skins, yoghurt, oil, lemon, maple syrup and salt for 1 minute in a food processor. Combine the peas with the chickpeas, then add the dressing. Stir and sprinkle with the chopped herbs.

ZUCCHINI QUINOA SALAD

Serves: 4 - Time: 40 minutes

YOU NEED

5 spring onions, finely sliced • 2 tablespoons extra virgin olive oil
185g red or white quinoa, or a mix of the two • 30g pine nuts, toasted
grated zest and juice of 1 lemon • 15g dried currants • 1 teaspoon salt, plus extra
to taste • 50g plain yoghurt • 2 zucchini or 6 baby zucchini, grated, green or
yellow, or a mix of the two • 2 handfuls of dill, chopped

18.4g
protein /
per serving
4 .6g

Fry the spring onions in 1 tablespoon oil until soft. Add the quinoa and pine
nuts and cook for 4 minutes. Add 370ml water, lemon zest, currants and a
pinch of salt. Boil then simmer for 15 minutes. Whisk the yoghurt, lemon juice,
1 tablespoon water, 1 teaspoon salt and remaining olive oil together. Combine
all the salad ingredients including the grated zucchini and the chopped dill.
Drizzle the yoghurt dressing over the top.

HAZELNUT, LENTIL & AVOCADO SALAD

Serves: 2 - Time: 45 minutes

YOU NEED

90g green lentils • 1 garlic clove, peeled • 30g hazelnuts, skinned

juice of 1 lemon • 1 teaspoon Dijon mustard

2 tablespoons extra virgin olive oil • 1 teaspoon honey

1 tablespoon white wine vinegar • salt and pepper to taste

1 avocado, peeled, stoned and sliced • a handful of parsley, chopped

Preheat the oven to 200°C/400°F. Put the lentils in a pan with 360ml water and the garlic, bring to the boil then simmer for 20 minutes. Remove the garlic. Meanwhile, roast the hazelnuts in the oven for 5 minutes. Whisk the lemon, mustard, oil, honey and vinegar until creamy, then set aside. Season with salt and pepper. Mix the avocado with the lentils and roasted nuts, add the parsley and stir through the dressing.

ASIAN AZUKI & MUNG BEAN SALAD

Serves: 4 - Time: 1 hour 25 minutes, plus soaking overnight

YOU NEED
180g dried azuki beans • 100g dried whole mung beans
5 tablespoons sesame oil • 4 garlic cloves, grated • 3–4 red or green chillies,
seeded and chopped • 3 spring onions, finely sliced • salt and pepper to taste
a handful of coriander, roughly chopped • juice of 1 lime

19.6g
protein /
per serving
4.9g

Soak the beans separately overnight, then drain and rinse. Put the beans in a large pan, cover with water and bring to the boil. Simmer for 40 minutes–1 hour until cooked, then drain. Fry the beans in 4 tablespoons of the oil with the garlic, chillies and spring onions for 5 minutes. Stir in the remaining oil then take the pan off the heat. Season with salt and pepper and serve with the chopped coriander and lime juice.

AZUKI BEAN & QUINOA TABBOULEH

Serves: 4 - Time: 30 minutes, plus soaking overnight (optional)

YOU NEED

90g dried azuki beans or 400g can, drained • 180g quinoa

2 large handfuls of parsley, roughly chopped

a large handful of mint, roughly chopped

3 medium tomatoes, seeded and cut into small cubes

1 cucumber, seeded and cut into small cubes • 25g pumpkin seeds

juice of ½ lemon • salt and pepper to taste

DRESSING

1 tablespoon red wine vinegar • 3 tablespoons extra virgin olive oil

1 garlic clove, grated • a small drizzle of maple syrup

30.6g
protein /
per serving
7.7g

If using dried beans, soak them overnight, then drain, put in a pan, cover with water and bring to the boil. Simmer for 45 minutes. Put the quinoa in a pan and cover with 360ml water. Boil, cover with a lid then simmer for 15 minutes. Put all the remaining ingredients, the beans and quinoa in a bowl, add the lemon juice and season with salt and pepper. Combine the dressing ingredients, season well, drizzle over the salad and serve.

EDAMAME & BARLEY SALAD

Serves: 4 - Time: 1 hour 15 minutes

YOU NEED

180g pearl barley • 3 tablespoons olive oil • 1 small red onion, finely chopped
salt and pepper to taste • 5 small beetroot • 2 teaspoons thyme leaves
3 tablespoons balsamic vinegar • 100g edamame beans, defrosted
40g toasted walnuts, chopped • 2 handfuls of parsley, chopped

Preheat the oven to 220°C/425°F. Cover the barley with water and cook for 20 minutes, then drain. While still warm, drizzle with 2 tablespoons olive oil, add the onion and season well with salt and pepper. Wrap the beetroot in foil with salt, thyme, vinegar and the remaining oil. Bake for 30 minutes. Once cooled peel off the skin, slice into quarters, add to the barley and stir well. Add the beans, walnuts and parsley, season and serve.

PISTACHIO-CRUSTED TOFU

Serves: 4 - Time: 50 minutes

YOU NEED

200g firm tofu, cut into 4 slices • 1½ tablespoons soy sauce • 45g pistachios
1 slice brown bread • 3 black peppercorns • 1 tablespoon Dijon mustard
1 tablespoon maple syrup • ½ tablespoon plain yoghurt • 1 egg yolk
olive oil, for drizzling

SALSA

½ red onion, sliced • 1 garlic clove, sliced • 1 tablespoon olive oil
salt and pepper to taste • 1 red capsicum, thinly sliced • 1 thyme sprig
½ tablespoon white wine vinegar • ½ tablespoon honey

Preheat the oven to 180°C/350°F. Brush the tofu with 1 tablespoon soy
sauce and set aside. Whizz the nuts, bread and peppercorns in a food processor
to fine crumbs. Combine the mustard, maple syrup, remaining soy sauce,
yoghurt and egg yolk, add the tofu and coat with the mixture, then coat the
tofu in the breadcrumb mix. Drizzle with oil and bake for 20 minutes. Fry the
onion and garlic in the oil and season. Add the capsicum and thyme and cook
for 8 minutes. Add the vinegar and honey and cook for 2 minutes.
Serve the tofu with the salsa.

TOFU, EGGPLANT & CHILLI SALAD

Serves: 4 - Time: 45 minutes

YOU NEED

60ml rice wine vinegar • 20g soft brown sugar • 1 teaspoon salt

1 teaspoon sesame oil • 2 garlic cloves, grated • 1 red chilli, finely chopped

3 baby eggplants, cut into small chunks • 2 tablespoons olive oil

200g firm tofu, cubed • 1 large ripe mango, cut into small chunks

4 spring onions, finely sliced • ½ red onion, thinly sliced

grated zest and juice of 1 lime • a handful of coriander leaves, roughly chopped

18.3g
protein /
per serving
4.6g

Combine the vinegar, sugar and salt in a pan and boil until the sugar has
dissolved. Take off the heat, add the sesame oil, garlic and chilli, then cool.
Fry the eggplant in batches in half the olive oil and drain on kitchen paper.
Do the same with the tofu. Combine everything together, except the coriander,
then stir in the cooled dressing. Sprinkle with coriander.

JAPANESE TUNA RICE SALAD

Serves: 4 - Time: 30 minutes

YOU NEED

100g edamame beans • 100g sugar snap peas, halved lengthways
300g brown rice, cooked • ½ cucumber, halved, seeded and thinly sliced
400g sushi-grade tuna, cut into 3mm slices • 40g pea shoots • 4 spring onions, sliced
4 tablespoons pickled ginger slices • 1 tablespoon black sesame seeds

---

DRESSING

1 tablespoon tamari • 2 tablespoons caster sugar
2 tablespoons rice vinegar • juice of 2 limes

142.8 g protein / per serving 37.2g

Combine the dressing ingredients. Cook the edamame beans and sugar snaps in boiling water for 2 minutes. Drain and rinse under cold water. Mix all the ingredients in a bowl except the sesame seeds, then pour over the dressing. Sprinkle with the sesame seeds and serve.

AVOCADO & ALMOND FARRO SALAD

Serves: 4 - Time: 1 hour 10 minutes

YOU NEED

200g farro • 1 garlic clove • 1 celery stick, cut in half • 1 carrot, cut in half
5 broccolini stems, cut into quarters • 8 medium asparagus
1 medium avocado, sliced • a small handful of mung bean sprouts
60g toasted blanched almonds • ¼ cucumber, cut into matchsticks
a handful of rocket

DRESSING

1 small garlic clove, grated • 2 tablespoons lemon juice • 4 tablespoons extra
virgin olive oil, plus extra for drizzling • salt and pepper to taste

26g
protein /
per serving
6.5g

Put the farro in a pan, cover with water and add the garlic, celery and carrot. Cook for 45 minutes, then drain. Combine the dressing ingredients, then stir into the farro. Cook the broccolini and asparagus for 4 minutes, drain and refresh under cold water. Add to the farro with the avocado and remaining ingredients. Drizzle with oil.

TARTS, CASSEROLES & SMALL DISHES

A collection of satisfying and easy to prepare recipes using a vast array of green proteins from chickpeas to soybeans to give you a wide range of flavours cooked in a variety of ways.

Moroccan vegetables & chickpeas • Lentil & red
bean chilli • Split pea casserole • Broad bean, pea &
asparagus bowl • Spicy red lentil dhal • Butter bean
& tomato stew • Warm farro bean stew • Cannellini
bean ratatouille • Kidney bean & tomato with eggs
Asparagus quinoa frittata • Rustic red capsicum
& tomato tart • Green galette with rocket pesto
Chickpea curry • Broad bean tagine • Cannellini
bean burgers • Zucchini & mung bean pilaf • Sweet
potato & mung bean tacos • Carrot & tofu soba
noodles • Griddled tempeh with beans • Crispy salt
& pink pepper tofu • Apple, lentil & barley risotto
Roasted lentil capsicum • Yellow dhal with spinach
Vegetable kebabs on bulgur

MOROCCAN VEGETABLES & CHICKPEAS

Serves: 4 - Time: 50 minutes

YOU NEED

1 red onion, quartered • 2 garlic cloves, grated

2 medium tomatoes, quartered • 200g butternut pumpkin, cut into chunks

1 medium carrot, cut into chunks • 1 red capsicum, cut into small chunks

½ teaspoon ground cinnamon • ½ teaspoon ground cumin

½ teaspoon cumin seeds • ½ teaspoon ground coriander

½ teaspoon ras el hanout (optional) • ½ teaspoon turmeric

salt and pepper to taste • 2 tablespoons olive oil • 250ml vegetable stock

400g can chickpeas, drained and rinsed • a handful of parsley, roughly chopped

---

HARISSA YOGHURT

100ml plain yoghurt • 1 tablespoon harissa paste

Preheat the oven to 220°C/425°F. Roast all the vegetables and spices, including salt and pepper, in the oil for 30 minutes, then put them in a pan and cover with stock. Boil then simmer and add the chickpeas. Cook for 10 minutes and season with salt and pepper to taste. Combine the yoghurt with the harissa. Sprinkle the vegetables with the parsley.

LENTIL & RED BEAN CHILLI

Serves: 4 - Time: 1 hour 10 minutes

YOU NEED

1 onion, finely chopped • 1 tablespoon olive oil

1 red capsicum, cut into small chunks • 1 garlic clove, grated

1 tablespoon ground chipotle peppers or 1 teaspoon chipotle paste

1 teaspoon hot chilli powder • 1 tablespoon ground cumin

1 teaspoon smoked paprika • 1 teaspoon ground coriander

½ teaspoon cayenne pepper • 1 bay leaf • 400g can chopped tomatoes

90g brown lentils • 90g red lentils

400g can red kidney beans, drained and rinsed • a drizzle of honey

salt and pepper to taste • a handful of coriander, roughly chopped

100g plain yoghurt • 1 small jalapeño, chopped

28g
protein /
per serving
7g

Fry the onion in the oil for 2 minutes. Add the red capsicum and garlic and fry for 1 minute. Add the spices and bay leaf and fry for 1 minute. Add the tomatoes, lentils, beans, 400ml water and honey and simmer for 50 minutes. Season with salt and pepper. Serve with the coriander, yoghurt and jalapeño.

SPLIT PEA CASSEROLE

Serves: 4 - Time: 1 hour 10 minutes

YOU NEED

180g dried yellow split peas, well rinsed • 1 tablespoon turmeric
1 teaspoon garam masala • 1 red onion, finely chopped • 1 teaspoon chilli powder
1 tablespoon olive oil • 1 garlic clove, grated • 2.5cm ginger, peeled and grated
½ head cauliflower, in florets • 200ml vegetable stock • 180g garden peas
½ red capsicum, seeded and chopped • 50g sultanas • 1 tomato, seeded and chopped

Cover the split peas with 700ml water, bring to the boil then simmer for
15 minutes. Drain. Fry the turmeric, garam masala, onion and chilli powder
in the oil for 1 minute. Add the garlic and ginger and fry for 30 seconds. Add
the cauliflower and stock and cook for 10 minutes. Add the split peas and stir
through. Add the remaining ingredients and cook for 5 minutes.

BROAD BEAN, PEA & ASPARAGUS BOWL

Serves 2 - Time: 35 minutes

YOU NEED

500ml vegetable stock • 150g orzo pasta

200g asparagus, trimmed and cut into 2cm pieces

100g frozen peas • 100g podded broad beans

a handful of basil leaves, torn • 2 tablespoons extra virgin olive oil

30g parmesan shavings

Pour the vegetable stock into a saucepan and bring to the boil. Add the orzo and cook for 7–10 minutes, then drain. Bring 500ml water to the boil in another saucepan, add the asparagus and cook for 3½ minutes. Remove the asparagus and add the peas to the water. Boil then add the broad beans for 30 seconds then drain. Mix the orzo and vegetables together, then add the basil and stir in the olive oil. Top with parmesan shavings.

SPICY RED LENTIL DHAL

Serves: 4 - Time: 50 minutes

YOU NEED

1 teaspoon cumin seeds • 1 teaspoon coriander seeds

2 teaspoons yellow mustard seeds • 1 teaspoon fenugreek seeds

½ teaspoon ground cinnamon • 1 teaspoon red chilli flakes

1 onion, finely chopped • 1 tablespoon olive oil • 2 garlic cloves, grated

2.5cm ginger, peeled and grated • 2 cardamom pods, seeded

1 litre vegetable stock • 1 tablespoon tomato purée • 220g red lentils

5 cherry tomatoes, chopped • juice of 1 lime

a handful of coriander, roughly chopped

Toast the seeds in a dry pan until they start to pop. Grind in a pestle and mortar and add the cinnamon and chilli. Fry the onion in the oil for 4 minutes, add the garlic, ginger and spices, including the cardamom and fry for 3 minutes. Add the stock, tomato purée and lentils. Boil then simmer for 20 minutes. Add the tomatoes, lime juice and coriander and cook for another 10 minutes.

BUTTER BEAN & TOMATO STEW

Serves: 4 - Time: 1 hour 30 minutes, plus soaking overnight (optional)

YOU NEED

225g dried butter beans or 450g can • 4 celery sticks, thinly sliced

1 tablespoon olive oil • 6 spring onions, thinly sliced • 4 garlic cloves, thinly sliced

1 teaspoon caraway seeds, lightly crushed • salt and pepper to taste

400g can plum tomatoes, drained, rinsed, cored and roughly chopped

10 pitted black olives, roughly chopped • 1 lemon, cut into quarters

18.8g protein / per serving 4.7g

If using dried beans, soak overnight, then drain and rinse. Fry the celery in the oil over a low heat for 10 minutes. Add half the spring onions, the garlic, caraway and 2 pinches of salt. Cook for 10 minutes on low. Add the tomatoes and cook for 2 minutes. Add the butter beans and 200ml water and simmer, covered, for 45 minutes. Season with salt and pepper. Top with the olives, remaining spring onions and lemon quarters.

WARM FARRO BEAN STEW

Serves: 4 - Time: 1 hour 20 minutes, plus soaking overnight

YOU NEED

200g pinto beans • 200g borlotti beans • 1 medium onion, roughly chopped
1 tablespoon olive oil • 2 x 400g cans chopped tomatoes
1 medium carrot, finely chopped • 3 small potatoes, chopped
2 celery sticks • 350g pearled farro • 500ml vegetable stock • 1 teaspoon salt
½ bunch kale, chopped • a handful of spinach leaves • 50g parmesan, grated
olive oil, for drizzling

Soak the beans overnight, then drain and rinse. Boil together in 1 litre water then simmer for 40 minutes. Drain and mash. Fry the onion in the oil for 3 minutes, add to the mashed beans with the tomatoes, carrot, potatoes, celery, farro and stock. Bring to the boil, then simmer for 20 minutes. Add the salt and stir in the kale and spinach, then simmer for 3 minutes. Sprinkle with grated parmesan and a drizzle of olive oil to serve.

CANNELLINI BEAN RATATOUILLE

Serves: 4 - Time: 1 hour 15 minutes, plus soaking overnight (optional)

YOU NEED

250g dried cannellini beans or 400g can

½ butternut pumpkin, cut into bite-sized chunks

1 red capsicum, cut into small chunks • 2 zucchini, cut into chunks

2 garlic cloves, grated • 5 tablespoons olive oil • 1 eggplant, cut into small chunks

1 red onion, roughly chopped • 1 tablespoon tomato purée

400g can plum tomatoes • 1 tablespoon white wine vinegar • 1 teaspoon honey

a handful of basil leaves

JALAPEÑO PESTO

1 tablespoon pickled jalapeño • 50g almonds • 1 garlic clove • 1 tablespoon parsley

30.5g protein / per serving 7.6g

If using dried beans, soak overnight, then drain and rinse. Cover with water, bring to the boil then simmer for 40 minutes. Preheat the oven to 220°C/425°F. Roast the pumpkin, capsicum, zucchini and garlic in 2 tablespoons oil for 30 minutes. Fry the eggplant in batches in 2 tablespoons oil until brown, then set aside. Fry the onion in 1 tablespoon oil until soft. Add the tomato purée and stir. Add the tomatoes, vinegar and honey and simmer for 10 minutes. Add the beans, roasted vegetables and eggplant and stir. Whizz all the pesto ingredients in a food processor for 30 seconds. Serve on top of the ratatouille and sprinkle with basil.

KIDNEY BEAN & TOMATO WITH EGGS

Serves: 4 - Time: 20 minutes

YOU NEED

1 red onion, finely chopped • 2 garlic cloves, grated • 1 tablespoon olive oil

½ teaspoon cumin seeds • ½ teaspoon ground cumin

¼ teaspoon chilli powder • 400g can red kidney beans, drained

4 firm ripe tomatoes, grated • 1 teaspoon salt

4 large eggs • a handful of coriander, finely chopped • 80ml plain yoghurt

Fry the onion and garlic in the oil over a low heat for 3 minutes. Add the spices
and cook for 1 minute. Add the beans and tomatoes, season with the salt and
cook for 5 minutes. Make 4 wells in the pan, and crack an egg into them.
Cover the pan to help the top of the eggs cook and cook for 4 minutes, or until
the eggs are cooked to your preference. Serve with coriander and yoghurt.

ASPARAGUS QUINOA FRITTATA

Serves: 4 - Time: 30 minutes

YOU NEED

2 leeks, sliced • 1 garlic clove, grated • 1 tablespoon olive oil

10 asparagus • 8 large eggs, beaten • 50g feta cheese

a handful of parsley, chopped, plus extra for sprinkling • a handful of baby spinach

100g quinoa, cooked • salt and pepper to taste

40g parmesan, grated, plus extra shaved parmesan for sprinkling

Fry the leeks and garlic in the oil in an ovenproof frying pan for 5 minutes.
Add the asparagus and cook for 4 minutes. Whisk the eggs, feta, parsley and
spinach together. Add the quinoa and season with salt and pepper. Add to
the pan and cook until browned underneath. Sprinkle the parmesan on top and
put under a hot grill for 3 minutes. Sprinkle with extra parsley and
shaved parmesan and serve.

RUSTIC RED CAPSICUM & TOMATO TART

Serves: 4 - Time: 35 minutes

YOU NEED

55g harissa paste • 55g ricotta • salt and pepper to taste

1 roasted red capsicum from a jar, sliced

10 cherry tomatoes, sliced • olive oil, for brushing

TART CRUST

55g chickpea (besan) flour • 110g plain flour

½ tablespoon baking powder • a pinch of salt

125ml lager • polenta, for dusting

Preheat the oven to 200°C/400°F. For the crust, combine the dry ingredients, add the beer and mix well. Dust a baking sheet with polenta and pat the dough out into a rustic pizza shape. Spread the harissa paste on the base. Add the ricotta and lightly season with salt and pepper to taste. Lay the capsicum and tomato slices on top. Fold over the edges of the tart and brush with oil.
Bake for 20 minutes.

GREEN GALETTE WITH ROCKET PESTO

Serves: 4 - Time: 45 minutes

YOU NEED

2 spring onions, thinly sliced • 1 tablespoon olive oil • 100g blanched almonds
2 large handfuls of rocket • 1 garlic clove • juice of 1 lemon
12 cherry tomatoes, halved and roasted for 30 minutes • 1 ripe avocado, sliced
100g feta, crumbled • 1 red chilli, sliced

GALETTE BASE

100g pistachios, shelled • 50g pumpkin seeds • 50g sunflower seeds
100g vacuum packed chestnuts • 1 tablespoon maple syrup • grated zest of 1 lemon
a small handful of thyme leaves • 1 tablespoon olive oil • salt and pepper to taste

77g
protein /
per serving
19.3g

Preheat the oven to 200°C/400°F. For the base, roast the nuts and seeds for
8 minutes. Whizz in a food processor with the chestnuts, maple syrup, lemon
zest, thyme, oil and season with salt and pepper. Shape the mixture into a 5mm
thick round on baking paper. Prick with a fork and bake for 20 minutes. Fry the
spring onions in the oil until soft. Whizz the almonds and rocket in a food
processor with the garlic, a pinch of salt and half the lemon juice. Spread the
rocket pesto over the galette, add the tomatoes, avocado, feta, chilli, remaining
lemon juice and the spring onions.

CHICKPEA CURRY

Serves: 4 - Time: 35 minutes

YOU NEED

1 teaspoon mustard seeds • 1 teaspoon turmeric • 2 teaspoons ground coriander

1 teaspoon fenugreek seeds • 1 teaspoon hot chilli powder • 1 tablespoon olive oil

1 onion, finely sliced • 1 tablespoon grated ginger • 2 garlic cloves, grated

2 x 400g cans chickpeas, drained and rinsed • 1 red capsicum, roughly chopped

6 tomatoes, seeded and roughly chopped

2 handfuls of curly kale, roughly chopped • 1 kaffir lime leaf

200g canned coconut milk • a handful of coriander leaves, roughly chopped

41.4g
protein /
per serving
10.3g

Fry the mustard seeds, turmeric, coriander, fenugreek and chilli powder in
the oil for 1 minute. Add the onion and fry for 2 minutes. Add the ginger and
garlic and fry for a few seconds. Add the chickpeas and capsicum and cook,
stirring, for 2 minutes then add the tomatoes. Cook for 2 minutes and add the
kale and lime leaf. Stir for 2 minutes then add the coconut milk and 100ml water.
Cover and cook for 5 minutes. Sprinkle with coriander.

BROAD BEAN TAGINE

Serves: 4 - Time: 1 hour 5 minutes

YOU NEED
½ red onion, roughly chopped • ½ tablespoon olive oil
½ garlic clove, finely chopped • ½ tablespoon grated ginger
½ teaspoon turmeric • ¼ teaspoon ground ginger
½ teaspoon ground cumin • 100g green lentils
150g broad beans, fresh or frozen • 4 artichokes, peeled and halved
½ preserved lemon, seeded and finely chopped • a handful of green olives
salt and pepper to taste • a handful of parsley, finely chopped
a handful of coriander, finely chopped

Fry the onion in the oil for 3 minutes. Add the garlic, ginger and spices and stir for 30 seconds. Add the lentils, cover with water, boil then simmer, covered, for 20 minutes. Add the beans, artichokes, lemon and olives and cover with more water. Boil, then simmer for 20 minutes; season with salt and pepper. Sprinkle with the herbs.

CANNELLINI BEAN BURGERS

Serves: 4 - Time: 50 minutes

YOU NEED

2 Portobello mushrooms, roughly chopped • ½ tablespoon thyme
1 tablespoon olive oil • salt and pepper to taste • 100g canned cannellini beans,
drained • 1 fresh date, pitted • 1 garlic clove, peeled • a handful of parsley
½ tablespoon tahini • ½ tablespoon soy sauce • 50g brown rice, cooked and cooled
25g brown breadcrumbs • grated zest of ¼ lemon • 2 brown buns, toasted

---

CUCUMBER PICKLE

½ cucumber, thinly sliced • 1 tablespoon white wine vinegar • 1 teaspoon honey

---

SPICED TAHINI SAUCE

2 tablespoons tahini • 2 teaspoons maple syrup • grated zest and juice of 1 lemon
4 tablespoons plain yoghurt • ¼ teaspoon harissa paste

12.5g
protein /
per serving
3g

Fry the mushrooms and thyme in the oil until they dry out slightly, season with salt and pepper. Whizz the beans, date, garlic, parsley, tahini and soy sauce in a food processor, then add the rice, breadcrumbs, lemon zest and mushrooms. Mix and chill for 10 minutes. Preheat the oven to 230°C/450°F. Divide the mixture into 4 patties, then bake for 15 minutes. Mix the cucumber with the vinegar, honey and salt to taste. Combine all the ingredients for the tahini sauce. Put the patties in the buns and serve with the pickle and tahini sauce.

ZUCCHINI & MUNG BEAN PILAF

Serves: 4 - Time: 30 minutes

YOU NEED

1 red onion, finely sliced • 4 tablespoons olive oil • salt and pepper to taste
2 zucchini, 1 cubed and 1 shaved • 1 teaspoon yellow mustard seeds
1 teaspoon fennel seeds • 180g dried mung beans • 180g brown basmati rice
400ml vegetable stock • 1 garlic clove, grated • a handful of pine nuts, toasted
a handful of raisins • a handful of parsley, roughly chopped
a handful of coriander, roughly chopped • 1 lemon

14.5g protein / per serving 3.6g

Sweat the onion in 1 tablespoon oil for 5 minutes with the lid on until soft. Season with salt and pepper. Fry the cubed zucchini in another tablespoon oil over a high heat until lightly browned, then add to the onion. Fry the mustard and fennel seeds in 1 tablespoon oil. Once popping add the mung beans and rice and stir. Add the stock and season. Boil, then simmer until the liquid has been absorbed. Fry the shaved zucchini in the remaining oil for a few minutes on each side until crispy. Combine everything together. Add the garlic, pine nuts, raisins, herbs and squeeze over the lemon.

SWEET POTATO & MUNG BEAN TACOS

Serves: 4 - Time: 55 minutes, plus 1 hour soaking

YOU NEED

1 large sweet potato or 2 small, peeled and cut into small chunks

1 small red onion, finely chopped • 1 tablespoon olive oil

1 teaspoon smoked paprika • 1 green capsicum, finely sliced

2 medium tomatoes, seeded and cubed • 200g canned chickpeas, drained and rinsed

1 teaspoon chipotle paste • 1 green chilli, finely chopped

a handful of coriander, roughly chopped • ½ lemon • 100ml plain yoghurt

---

MUNG BEAN TACOS

100g red lentils • 100g whole mung beans • 1 garlic clove, grated

½ teaspoon ground cumin • ½ teaspoon cumin seeds • 1½ teaspoons salt

2 tablespoons olive oil, for frying

25g
protein /
per serving
6.3g

For the tacos, soak the lentils and mung beans in 230ml water for 1 hour. Drain and whizz in a food processor with the remaining ingredients for 1 minute. If you feel that the batter is too thick add 1–2 tablespoons water (it should be the consistency of pancake batter). Preheat the oven to 200°C/400°F. Roast the sweet potato for 25 minutes. Heat the 2 tablespoons oil in a pan, add a tablespoonful of the batter and cook for 3 minutes on each side. Repeat to make 8. Fry the onion in the oil for 2 minutes. Add the paprika, capsicum, tomatoes, chickpeas and chipotle paste and cook for 2 minutes. Add the sweet potato and combine, then fill the tacos with the mixture. Sprinkle the chilli, coriander and lemon juice over the tacos with the yoghurt.

CARROT & TOFU SOBA NOODLES

Serves: 4 - Time: 1 hour 30 minutes

YOU NEED

4 tablespoons white wine vinegar • 1 tablespoon honey

1 teaspoon salt • 1 red onion, thinly sliced • 3 tablespoons smooth peanut butter

1 teaspoon soy sauce • juice of ½ lime • 3 teaspoons sesame oil

1 teaspoon fish sauce • 1 teaspoon maple syrup

200g soba noodles, cooked and cooled • 500g firm tofu, cut into bite-sized cubes

2 tablespoons olive oil • 2 spring onions, finely sliced

2 carrots, cut into matchsticks • 100g beansprouts • a handful of coriander, chopped

1 teaspoon black sesame seeds

Whisk the vinegar and honey with the salt until the salt has dissolved. Add the onion and leave for 1 hour. Whisk the peanut butter with the soy sauce, lime juice, sesame oil, fish sauce, maple syrup and 1 tablespoon water. Add the noodles. Fry the tofu in 1 tablespoon oil until browned; set aside. Fry the spring onions and carrots in the remaining oil for 2 minutes. Add the beansprouts and fry for 2 minutes. Add the tofu with the noodles and vegetables. Serve with the pickled onion, coriander and sesame seeds.

GRIDDLED TEMPEH WITH BEANS

Serves: 4 - Time: 20 minutes, plus 30 minutes marinating

YOU NEED

225g tempeh • 3 tablespoons soy sauce • 3 tablespoons maple syrup
1 teaspoon chipotle paste • 1 teaspoon rice vinegar • 1 garlic clove, grated
200g green beans, topped • 1 shallot, finely chopped
1 tablespoon black sesame seeds • 1 tablespoon olive oil, for drizzling
salt and pepper to taste

Cut the tempeh into 4 slices and again in half. Combine the soy sauce, maple syrup, chipotle and vinegar with the garlic in a bowl. Marinate the tempeh for 30 minutes. Boil the beans for 5 minutes until tender. Meanwhile, preheat a griddle pan and grill the tempeh brushing with the marinade for 3 minutes on each side. Drain the beans, stir through the shallot and sesame seeds, then drizzle with oil and season with salt and pepper. Serve with the tempeh.

CRISPY SALT & PINK PEPPER TOFU

Serves: 4 - Time: 25 minutes

YOU NEED

1 teaspoon pink peppercorns, roughly ground • 3 tablespoons cornflour
½ teaspoon salt • 2 tablespoons flavourless oil • 225g block of extra firm tofu, sliced
½ cucumber, cut into batons • 50g beansprouts
150g iceberg lettuce, shredded
1 carrot, cut into julienne • a small handful of coriander leaves
a small handful of mint leaves

DIPPING SAUCE

1 red chilli, chopped • 1 garlic clove, grated • 2 tablespoons lime juice
4 tablespoons fish sauce • 3 teaspoons honey

33.8g
protein /
per serving
8.5g

Combine the pink peppercorns, cornflour and salt in a shallow dish.
Heat the oil in a pan. Coat the tofu in the cornflour mix, then fry gently
in batches for 5 minutes on each side until crispy. Mix together the dipping
sauce ingredients. Combine all the vegetables and herbs in another bowl. Serve
the tofu on top of the vegetables with the sauce.

APPLE, LENTIL & BARLEY RISOTTO

Serves: 4 - Time: 1 hour 20 minutes

YOU NEED

1 celeriac, peeled and cut into small chunks • 2 thyme sprigs

3 tablespoons olive oil • 1 large onion, finely chopped

1 apple, cored, peeled and cubed • 2 bay leaves • 175g green lentils

175g barley • 100ml white wine • 1 egg yolk • 1 teaspoon wholegrain mustard

4 tablespoons grated parmesan • 2 tablespoons plain yoghurt

2 tablespoons butter, melted • a handful of parsley, roughly chopped

35.5g
protein /
per serving
8.9g

Preheat the oven to 220°C/425°F and line a baking tray with greaseproof paper. Put the celeriac on the baking tray, sprinkle over the thyme and 1 tablespoon oil and roast for 40 minutes. Fry the onion in the remaining oil for 2 minutes. Add the apple and cook for 1 minute. Add the bay leaves, lentils, barley and wine and add water to cover. Boil, then simmer for 25 minutes. Combine the egg yolk with the mustard, parmesan and yoghurt. Mix the roasted celeriac, melted butter and cheesy yoghurt mixture together, then stir into the risotto and sprinkle with parsley.

ROASTED LENTIL CAPSICUM

Serves: 4 - Time: 55 minutes

YOU NEED

2 red capsicums • 100g red or green lentils, cooked • 1 garlic clove, sliced
2 anchovy fillets from a jar, chopped • 50g feta, crumbled
2 medium tomatoes, seeded and chopped • salt and pepper to taste
a handful of basil leaves • 2 tablespoons olive oil

Preheat the oven to 200°C/400°F. Cut the capsicum in half and remove the stalk and seeds. Put 2 tablespoons of lentils in each capsicum half. Divide the garlic between each capsicum half and add the anchovies. Add the feta and top with tomatoes, then season with salt and pepper to taste. Cover the capsicum with foil and roast for 25 minutes, then uncover and roast for 15 minutes until cooked. Whizz the basil and oil in a food processor for 1 minute. Drizzle the capsicum with the basil oil.

YELLOW DHAL WITH SPINACH

Serves: 4 - Time: 45 minutes

YOU NEED

2 teaspoons mustard seeds • 1 tablespoon olive oil • 1 teaspoon chilli flakes
¼ teaspoon fenugreek seeds • 8 curry leaves • 1 small red onion, finely chopped
a thumb-sized piece ginger, peeled and grated • 2 garlic cloves, grated
1 tomato, chopped • 300g baby spinach leaves • a handful of coriander, chopped

---

DHAL

200g yellow split peas • ½ teaspoon turmeric
a thumb-sized piece ginger, peeled and grated • salt and pepper to taste

24.7g
protein /
per serving
6.2g

For the dhal, put the split peas, 500ml water, turmeric and ginger in a pan and
bring to the boil, then simmer for 25 minutes. When cooked, season with salt
and pepper. Fry the mustard seeds in the oil until they pop. Add the chilli flakes,
fenugreek seeds and curry leaves and cook for 20 seconds. Add the onion,
ginger and garlic and cook for 1 minute. Add the tomato and spinach and
cook for 2 minutes. Tip into the dhal and add the coriander.

VEGETABLE KEBABS ON BULGUR

Serves: 2 - Time: 1 hour 20 minutes, plus 30 minutes soaking

YOU NEED

1 zucchini, cut into bite-sized chunks • 1 eggplant, cut into bite-sized chunks
1 red capsicum, cut into chunks • 1 red onion, cut into quarters
8 cherry tomatoes • olive oil, for drizzling • salt and pepper to taste
100g bulgur wheat • 100g quinoa • 50g pine nuts, toasted
a handful of parsley, roughly chopped

PESTO

50g blanched almonds, toasted • 3 garlic cloves • 125ml extra virgin olive oil
125ml groundnut oil • 70g mint leaves • 30g parsley leaves • 2 teaspoons honey
juice of ½ lemon

12.5g
protein /
per serving
6.3g

Soak 8 wooden skewers for at least 30 minutes. Thread the vegetables onto
the skewers, drizzle with oil and season with salt and pepper. Cook for
15 minutes on a preheated griddle pan or hot barbecue. Cover the bulgur
wheat with 100ml boiling water and leave for 20 minutes. Put the quinoa in a pan,
cover with 200ml cold water and cook, covered, for 15 minutes, then drain.
Combine both grains with the pine nuts, parsley and seasoning, then drizzle
with oil. Whizz the pesto ingredients in a food processor for 1 minute. Serve the
kebabs on the bulgur with the pesto.

DESSERTS

Chocolate brownies never tasted so good when using special ingredients like azuki beans. Enjoy the sweet side of protein knowing how good these treats are for you.

Chocolate & chickpea torte • Chocolate & cashew azuki bites • Date & orange quinoa scones • Dark berry quinoa nut bowl • Spiced apple quinoa muffins • Pecan waffles with strawberries • Blueberry, mint & tofu smoothie • Tofu & banana French toasts Chocolate & ginger ice-cream • Cardamom spiced cookies • Azuki bean & walnut brownies

CHOCOLATE & CHICKPEA TORTE

Serves: 8–10 - Time: 1 hour 10 minutes

YOU NEED

200g dark chocolate (70% cocoa solids), broken into squares

150g icing sugar, sifted • 150g unsalted butter, softened

400g can chickpeas, drained and rinsed • 3 medium eggs, separated

chopped pistachios and cocoa powder, for dusting

48.5 g
protein /
per serving
12.1g

Preheat the oven to 190°C/375°F and line a 23cm springform cake tin with greaseproof paper. Melt the chocolate in a heatproof bowl set over a pan of simmering water, stir, then cool. Whizz the sugar, butter and chickpeas in a food processor to form a heavy batter. Add the egg yolks and blend. Add the chocolate and stir to combine. Whisk the egg whites until stiff but not dry. Fold into the chocolate mixture and spoon into the tin. Bake for 35 minutes. Cool before serving then sprinkle with chopped pistachios and dust with cocoa powder.

CHOCOLATE & CASHEW AZUKI BITES

Makes about 12 - Time: 1 hour 15 minutes, plus 4 hours soaking and 1 hour chilling

YOU NEED

115g dried azuki beans • 75g pecans

6 medjool dates • ¼ teaspoon cocoa powder • 1 teaspoon maple syrup

¼ teaspoon vanilla extract • 1¼ teaspoons salt

140g cashews, finely chopped

Soak the beans for 4 hours, then drain, cover with water and boil for 1 hour. Drain and cool slightly. Whizz the beans, pecans, dates, cocoa, maple syrup, vanilla and ¼ teaspoon salt in a food processor until smooth. If dry add a little water. Scoop out the dough with a tablespoon and roll into a ball; repeat to make 12. Combine the cashews and remaining salt then roll the balls in the mix. Chill for 1 hour.

DATE & ORANGE QUINOA SCONES

Makes 12 - Time: 30 minutes

YOU NEED
130g plain flour • 130g quinoa flour • 40g caster sugar • 1 teaspoon salt
1½ teaspoons baking powder • ½ teaspoon bicarbonate of soda
115g unsalted butter, cubed • 2 teaspoons grated orange zest
50g chopped dates • 120ml buttermilk, plus extra for brushing

19.9g
protein /
per serving
5g

Preheat the oven to 220°C/425°F and line a baking tray with greaseproof paper. Sift the dry ingredients, then rub in the butter until it resembles breadcrumbs. Add the zest and dates and toss to coat. Add the buttermilk to the dough until it holds together. Turn out on a floured board and roll to a 2cm thickness. Using a 5cm round cutter, cut the dough into 12 scones. Place the scones on the baking tray and brush with a little buttermilk. Bake for 12 minutes until golden. Cool on a wire rack.

DARK BERRY QUINOA NUT BOWL

Serves: 4 - Time: 25 minutes

YOU NEED
240ml almond milk • 190g quinoa, red or white • 140g blackberries
140g blueberries • ½ teaspoon ground cinnamon • 4 teaspoons runny honey
40g pecans, toasted and chopped

14.8g
protein /
per serving
3.7g

Bring the milk, 240ml water and quinoa to the boil, then simmer for 15 minutes
until most of the liquid has been absorbed. Take off the heat and leave for
5 minutes. Stir in the fruit with the cinnamon and honey. Sprinkle with pecans.

SPICED APPLE QUINOA MUFFINS

Makes 10 muffins - Time: 50 minutes

YOU NEED

150g unsalted butter • 2–3 large apples, cored and diced

1 teaspoon ground cinnamon • ½ teaspoon ground ginger

½ teaspoon ground nutmeg • 110g brown sugar • 1 egg

½ teaspoon vanilla extract • a pinch of salt • 1 teaspoon baking powder

185g quinoa, cooked and cooled • 160g plain flour • 60ml milk

40g chopped walnuts

26.7g
protein /
per serving
6.8g

Preheat the oven to 190°C/375°F and grease a muffin tin. In a frying pan, heat 2 tablespoons butter, add the apples and spices, stir to coat and cook until softened. Beat the remaining butter and sugar until light and creamy. Add the egg and beat until pale and fluffy. Beat in the vanilla, salt and baking powder. Fold in the apples and quinoa, add the flour and milk and stir. Divide the batter into the muffin tin. Top with the walnuts and bake for 25 minutes. Cool in the tin for 5 minutes then put on a wire rack to cool.

PECAN WAFFLES WITH STRAWBERRIES

Serves: 4 - Time: 35 minutes

YOU NEED

175g wholewheat flour • 140g rye flour • 2 tablespoons brown sugar
1 teaspoon salt • 1 tablespoon baking powder • 430ml soy milk
1 tablespoon vanilla extract • 2 eggs, lightly beaten • 4 tablespoons butter, melted
grated zest of ½ orange • 50g pecans, chopped, plus extra for sprinkling
100g strawberries • 100ml plain yoghurt

62.8g
protein /
per serving
15.7g

Combine the flours, sugar, salt and baking powder. Stir in the milk, vanilla and
eggs, with the butter. Add the orange zest and pecans and stir to combine.
Spoon 120ml of batter into a waffle iron and cook according to the machine's
instructions. Serve with the strawberries, extra pecans and yoghurt.

BLUEBERRY, MINT & TOFU SMOOTHIE

Serves: 1 - Time: 5 minutes

YOU NEED

75g blueberries • a small handful of mint leaves

150ml unsweetened almond milk • 60g silken tofu

½ tablespoon honey

Put all the ingredients into a blender and whizz for about 1 minute. If you
prefer it sweeter, add a little more honey.

TOFU & BANANA FRENCH TOASTS

Serves: 2 - Time: 25 minutes

YOU NEED
115g silken tofu • 30ml soy milk • ½ teaspoon vanilla extract
½ teaspoon ground cinnamon • 4 slices brioche, sliced
1 banana, diagonally sliced • 2 tablespoons unsalted butter
icing sugar, for dusting

13.2g
protein /
per serving
6.6g

Whizz the tofu, milk, vanilla, cinnamon and 30ml water in a blender for
1 minute. Pour into a shallow bowl. Make 2 sandwiches using the brioche
and fill with banana, then put each sandwich in the tofu mixture and leave for
30 seconds on each side. Heat a frying pan and add the butter. Brown one
sandwich for 4 minutes on each side. Repeat. Cut in half and sprinkle with
icing sugar. Serve with maple syrup.

CHOCOLATE & GINGER ICE-CREAM

Serves: 4 - Time: 1 hour 10 minutes, plus 1 hour chilling

YOU NEED

490ml soy milk • 35g cocoa powder

60g dark chocolate (at least 70% cocoa solids), broken into pieces

4 large egg yolks • 180g caster sugar • ¾ teaspoon vanilla extract

50g stem ginger, cut into small squares • 1 tablespoon stem ginger syrup

45.2g
protein /
per serving
11.3g

Heat the milk and cocoa slowly until boiling. Add the chocolate, take off the heat and whisk until the chocolate has melted. Whisk the eggs with the sugar. Add the warm milk and keep whisking. Add the vanilla, ginger and syrup, then pour everything back into the pan and heat over a medium–low heat until it's 79°C/174°F, then leave on the heat for 25 seconds. Strain the mixture and cool. Once cooled, chill for an hour, then churn in an ice-cream machine for 30–40 minutes. Serve.

CARDAMOM SPICED COOKIES

Makes 15 - Time: 35 minutes

YOU NEED

140g plain flour • 1 teaspoon ground cardamom • ½ teaspoon salt
¼ teaspoon baking powder • 2 large eggs • 135g caster sugar
75g ground almonds • 15 whole almonds

40g
protein /
per serving
10g

Preheat the oven to 180°C/350°F and line a baking tray with greaseproof
paper. Sift the flour, cardamom, salt and baking powder into a bowl. Beat
the eggs with the sugar until light and creamy. Stir the flour mixture into the
egg mixture and add the ground almonds. Stir to form a dough. Pinch a small
piece of dough to create a 2.5cm ball and flatten slightly. Press a whole almond
into the centre and repeat. Bake for 12 minutes. Cool on a wire rack.

AZUKI BEAN & WALNUT BROWNIES

Makes 12–16 - Time: 35 minutes

YOU NEED

400g can azuki beans, drained • 85g dark brown sugar • 30g cocoa powder

7 tablespoons vegetable oil • ¼ teaspoon salt • 2 medium eggs

8 squares dark chocolate, broken into small pieces • 50g walnuts, halved

Preheat the oven to 180°C/350°F. Line a 20cm square baking tin with baking paper. Whizz everything, except the chocolate and nuts, in a food processor for 1 minute. Fold through the walnuts and chocolate and pour into the tin. Bake for 20–25 minutes. Cool on a wire rack until it becomes fudge-like.

GLOSSARY OF TERMS

Amino acids – These are organic compounds that combine to form proteins.

Animal protein – Animal sources of protein include meats, dairy products, fish and eggs.

Antioxidant – These are man-made or natural substances that may prevent or delay some types of cell damage. They are found in many foods including fruits and vegetables.

Enzymes – These are complex proteins that cause a specific chemical change in all parts of the body.

Essential amino acids – This group of amino acids cannot be made by the body, so they have to come from our food. There are nine in total: histidine, isoleucine, leucine, lysine, methionine, phenylalanine, threonine, tryptophan and valine.

Glycaemic index – Or GI, measures how a carbohydrate-containing food raises blood glucose level. A food with a high GI raises blood glucose more than a food with a medium or low GI. Meats and fats do not have a GI because they do not contain carbohydrates.

Non-essential amino acids – These are amino acids which are produced by our body. They include alanine, asparagine, aspartic acid and glutamic acid.

Plant proteins – These sources of protein include whole grains, pulses, legumes, soy, nuts and seeds.

Phytochemicals – These are beneficial nutrients provided by plant food which help protect against cancer.

Protein – These are the building blocks of life and every cell in the human body contains them. The basic structure of protein is a long chain of amino acids.

INDEX

Published in Australia and New Zealand in 2015
by Hachette Australia
(an imprint of Hachette Australia Pty Limited)
Level 17, 207 Kent Street, Sydney NSW 2000
www.hachette.com.au

10 9 8 7 6 5 4 3 2 1

Cataloguing-in-Publication data is available from
the National Library of Australia.

978 0 7336 3418 5 (pbk.)

Acknowledgements

Thank you to my dear friend Louisa for our endless foodie chats and unconditional advice. Thank you very much M&M for your constant encouragement; not sure what I would do without it.

UK Publisher: Catie Ziller   **Author:** Fern Green
Photographer: Deirdre Rooney   **Designer:** Michelle Tilly
Editor: Kathy Steer

Printed in China by Toppan Leefung Printing Limited